Scottish History

A Concise Overview of the History of Scotland From Start to End

Eric Brown

© Copyright 2019 by Eric Brown - All rights reserved.

The following eBook is reproduced below with the goal of providing information that is as accurate and reliable as possible. Regardless, purchasing this eBook can be seen as consent to the fact that both the publisher and the author of this book are in no way experts on the topics discussed within and that any recommendations or suggestions that are made herein are for entertainment purposes only. Professionals should be consulted as needed prior to undertaking any of the action endorsed herein.

This declaration is deemed fair and valid by both the American Bar Association and the Committee of Publishers Association and is legally binding throughout the United States.

Furthermore, the transmission, duplication or reproduction of any of the following work including specific information will be considered an illegal act irrespective of if it is done electronically or in print. This extends to creating a secondary or tertiary copy of the work or a recorded copy and is only allowed with an expressed written consent from the Publisher.

All additional rights reserved.

The information in the following pages is broadly considered to be a truthful and accurate account of facts, and as such any inattention, use or misuse of the information in question by the reader will render any resulting actions solely under their purview. There are no scenarios in which the publisher or the original author of this work can be in any fashion deemed liable for any hardship or damages that may befall them after undertaking information described herein.

Additionally, the information in the following pages is intended only for informational purposes and should thus be thought of as universal.

As befitting its nature, it is presented without assurance regarding its prolonged validity or interim quality. Trademarks that are mentioned are done without written consent and can in no way be considered an endorsement from the trademark holder.

Table of Contents

Introduction 5

Chapter 1: Early Scotland 7

Chapter 2: The Golden Age 12

Chapter 3: The Emergence of the Scottish Nation State 33

Chapter 4: The Wars of Independence 41

Chapter 5: The Black Death 80

Chapter 6: How Scotland Was Built Into An Industrial Economy By Inventors, Explorers, And Missionaries 84

Chapter 7: Problems Facing Scotland Today 91

Conclusion 94

Introduction

The very idea of Scottishness is inseparable from an opposition to Englishness. England's influence on its northern neighbor, after it became the most powerful political force in the British Isles by 1100 cannot be understated.

However, Scotland has long insisted on being a separate country on a shared Island. Historical fact and myth had been resolutely channeled into the creation of a distinct national identity over the centuries. For the majority of human history. However, there was no Scotland, Wales, Ireland or England to speak of. Scotland is derived from the Latin scope here, which means Land of the Scots.

The Scots were a Celtic people of Irish origins, who decided to settle on the west coast of Great Britain during the fifth century AD. The people who habit Skoda, which only meant the entire kingdom North of England during Alexander the second's rain, were certainly not monolingual or monocultural. As the Scottish language slowly became the lingua franca of the entire nation, it had to coexist with Celtic, Gaelic and Norwegian.

Before a national identity was forged through the trauma of invasion and years of painful resistance, local, regional and dynastic identities and affiliation had more meaning and relevance to everyone's daily lives. When roads and advanced technologies for communication did not exist, everyone's existence was rooted in their immediate surroundings. Identities were formed based on the specific physical geography that individuals, families and clans found themselves in.

Scotland's terrain is mostly rugged, and subject to weather extremes but this challenging landscape also possesses a striking beauty and the capacity to facilitate the evolution of a fiercely unique culture. Scottish folklore has perpetuated the idea that the Scots have never been conquered. The Scots have certainly fought bravely against conquest from various foreign powers, but they also have a mixed track record.

It is true that the Romans eventually abandon their attempts to conquer Scotland, which was then known as Caledonia. And decided to simply build walls to keep the barbaric tribes up north from attacking them. In the 10th century, the Scots managed to fend off a Danish invasion, but only with English aid. This dependency meant that the English ruler could define himself as father and Lord of the king of Scots.

Chapter 1: Early Scotland

To envision what Scotland's earliest history looked like. You must make an effort to consciously imagine a time long before there was a heavily urbanized population. There were no road networks in existence, or a string of towns and cities connected by frequent trade. The forests were all unclear, and bogs were filled to the brim, and the heavily mountainous terrain prevented easy migrations up, down and across the lands. The Highlands to the north and west, which contained most of Scotland's hills. And mountains were far less hospitable than the flatter and more fertile lowlands to the south and east. Most long distance travel and trade would have been achieved by water along Scotland's 10 major rivers, numerous forts and its extensive coastline.

The majority of Scotland's earliest inhabitants toiled in one form of agriculture or another, helping to ensure that their local area could produce all the food and goods it needed to be self-sufficient. One's wealth and happiness largely dependent on the fertility of the land that one had access to. As well as one's industriousness in extracting subsistence from it. The Scottish terrain only became inhabitable to people towards the end of the last glacial period, circa 115,000 to circa 11,700 years ago. Much of North America was blanketed by ice during this time, while the Scandinavian ice sheet extended its reach into the northern British Isles. As the ice made its final retreat northward in approximately 7000 BC Mesolithic foragers' journey northward to access the green pastures it left in its wake. Little is known about the earliest of Scotland's inhabitants, since they left little archaeological evidence behind.

A Greek Mariner left behind the first written reference to Scotland in about 320 BC. Piteous referred to the northern part of the British Isles with the name orcas. A Celtic word that was most probably derived from the name of a local tribe he encountered during his travels. It means the young boars and lives on in modern times as Orkney a rugged archipelago off Scotland's northeastern coast. It also provides evidence that Celtic speakers were present that far up north by fourth century BC. The earliest extensive historical record dates to Rome's first encounter with medieval Scotland. The feared Roman legions arrived towards the end of the first century AD, after they successfully conquered the Celtic tribes of England and Wales after three decades of subjugation. Like their Southern counterparts, the inhabitants of Scotland, or Caledonia, as the Romans referred to it then, mostly spoke a form of Celtic language. Unlike Southern Britain, however, Caledonia's fierce warrior tribes would mount an effective resistance against the mighty Roman Empire.

Roman ambitions to access Scotland's lead, silver and gold with plans to enrich it further by enslaving the Scottish tribes and forcing them to pay taxes would eventually be thwarted. By the time the Romans first encountered Scotland, a chief dumb society. Which was more hierarchical and unequal had emerged. Large underground stores, Sioux terrains were a contributor to this social inequality, allowing local chiefs to hoard surplus crops and resources they had extracted from the land. Hierarchies within Scottish settlements gave way to hierarchies between settlements as tribes, which each consisted of a few thousand members vied with each other for power and control over resources. In the presence of a foreign common enemy, the warring tribes united to defend their homeland. In 79 AD, the Roman governor led the first incursion into Caledonia. After a few campaigns, the Romans achieved a decisive victory in 83 A.D at the Battle of Mons Gropius.

General Julius Agra cola defeated the Caledonians there. They were fighting under the leadership of Cowdicas, a chieftain of the Caledonian Confederacy. When their initial vision of conquering the entire British Isles was finally at hand, however, the Roman military found that their attention was needed in other parts of their empire. To safeguard Rome's glorious conquest of Southern Britain against the fierce Scottish warriors. The Romans built Hadrian's Wall on the time Solvay line in the 120s and 130s. During the middle of the second century, a second wall, N-9 wall was built on the fourth Clyde line. This re-occupation only lasted for roughly a decade. After briefly including Southern Scotland within the Roman province of Britannia. The Romans eventually gave up their campaign against tribes, which were unsharedable described as the barbarians from the north. And relatively idealized as the last men on Earth, the last of the free.

They retreated to Hadrian's Wall. Roman presence was maintained in the southwest part of Scotland, near Hadrian's Wall until the decline of the Roman Empire. Despite Rome's aborted conquest of Scotland, its empire left behind a profound influence on the inhabitants of Caledonia. The duality was not entirely between the Imperial Roman and the oppressed native, but between those who were within and outside the mighty Empire. The inhabitants of the British Isles had the opportunity to join the Roman army for their own gain. While others undoubtedly saw the benefits of aligning themselves with the most extensive political and social entity in the West. Like all imperial powers, Rome impacted the locals through a combination of hard and soft power.

Apart from their military prowess, they came with Roman commodities, luxury items and wealth that could be used to seduce local leaders to their cause. The rivaling warrior chiefs were thus incentivized to take advantage of Roman resources to get a competitive edge over their rivals. When they came face to face with the various trade objects that circulated through Rome's international economic system. The Caledonian inevitably realized that they were isolated from an international highway of ideas, trade and cultural exchange. Room's most lasting effect on the Caledonians is undoubtedly the introduction of Christianity.

The religion of the Empire slowly extended its influence up north, reaching places and communities that the Roman military would not. Much of the evangelizing work was probably done by British and Irish missionaries, who were intent on converting the northern pagans to their cause. The new religion came with new trade links to the Irish Sea and Atlantic Gaul, which provided the foreign objects necessary for the new Christians to conduct their rituals of faith. These were pottery designed to contain wine and oil, which were inevitably accompanied by new aesthetic and intellectual conceptions.

Chapter 2: The Golden Age

The earliest evidence of mankind in Scotland, dates to the Meso lithic or Middle Stone Age after the glaciers melted. This was a period of transition between the hunting and gathering of the proceeding Old Stone Age. The agricultural development of the New Stone Age was yet to come. At this time, Scotland was mainly a woodland region. Its occupants hunted wild pigs, red and roe deer, new sources of food gathering were also found. Catching birds, fishing and gathering nuts, fruits and shellfish. Settlements during this period are found on the coast and along rivers. Tools made of bone antler, flint and stone were used. Barb's made of tiny Flint blades hafted to wooden shafts were commonly used. Bone was used to make harpoons and fish hooks. The large number of fish bones excavated suggests that boats were used in fishing even though no boats from this period had been found. There were likely dugout canoes like ones found in England.

The best known of these early excavated sites is at Morton on Tensmere north of Saint Andrew's. Other sites include Dundee and Broadly ferry on Bayside. On the isles of Rum and Orinsay, Campbeltown and Oban in Argyle along the River D. Ethan Rivers in Grampian, re-point unlock Tardan and several sites along the banks of the fourth and Clyde. The Neolithic or New Stone Age was the period the plow was developed and farming began. Scotland's woodlands were cleared and wheat and barley were planted. Sheep, goats, pigs, cattle and dogs were all domesticated. With farming came a settled way of life, which allowed for new developments like pottery. The first pots were simply built by using coils of clay. The bucket shaped elaborately decorated, grooved wear was to follow. Also, Shell and bone beads were developed during the New Stone Age.

The focus of archeological study during this period is the megalithic monuments rather than stone tools. Tombs, standing stones and stone circles all dotted the landscape. During this time, Flint tools continued to be used and were fashioned into arrowheads, knives and axes. Tools designed for woodworking were also found, as well as clothing fasteners made from jet and bone pins. Early farmers lived in farmsteads occupied by one or two families such as Nap of Hauer and

Petty Garth's field. Later small communities were found such as Skara Brae and Barn house in the Orkney Islands.

In northern Scotland. Houses were made of stone and stone built field walls have been found. Larger buildings such as Danny Dale Temple on Shetlands mainland may have been used as communal meeting places. In central and southern Scotland. Houses and fences were made of timber rather than stone. Large Neolithic timber halls have been discovered at bell Brady in Grampian and town head on the isle of Butte. Some of the larger communities may have developed a specialization of labor allowing some individuals to work solely as carpenters, fishers or stone workers. An axe factory has been identified at Killen in Perthser. Stone circles are found in all parts of Scotland with concentrations in the North East, South West, and Outer Hebrides. They were likely used as meeting places for rituals and ceremonies.

Perhaps the best known is the 12 apostles at Dumfries, which is the largest stone circle in Scotland and the fifth largest in Britain. Some stones in Scotland have other arrangements aside from circles. There is a horse shoe arrangement at Asha vantage and a fan shaped arrangement at Hill of many stains, which may have originally included 600 stones. Hinges are circular earthworks comprising a bank and a ditch. These are only found in Britain. Entry into the center is gained by a causeway across the ditch and passage through the bank.

Hinges are believed to have been gathering places for ritual ceremonies. Often hinges have stone circles within the center like the one had Karen People in West Lithion. Others like the one at Belford hinge in Fife had timber circles.

Many stone tombs from this period can be found across Scotland. There are many chambered tombs in Scotland. The grandness of these is Maize Hall on the Orkney Mainland. Some with a passage leading to a small chamber such as Univac at North West. Others are large like Midhow on Rousse, which is divided into 12 chambers. Some chambered tombs like Trevor so tweak on Rousse have double story chambers. Long Barrow Tombs are comprised of a turf and stone mound like Keapo, Kencardine. Bronze is made by melting together copper and tin. Scotland has natural copper deposits, but the tin needed to have come from elsewhere like Devon and Cornwall. Gold items in Scotland are not native, but have been thought to have come from Ireland.

The beaker culture named for their large beaker drinking vessels made their way to Scotland at this time. The beaker people first appeared in southern Britain in 2,750 BC. This was a time when the first weapons like swords and spears appeared in Scotland. Weapons have been found in hoards, deposited in rivers are locks such as the hoard found in Dunstan lock Edinburgh. Bronze items were also made for domestic use such as knives, razors, chisels, sickles, pins and cauldrons. Woven woolen cloth and leather was used to make clothes. Both men and women dressed in tunics, skirts and shirts like garments with hats commonly worn. There was a division of labor. Most people farmed, but there would have been a local Bron Smith, minors, carpenters, potters and traders. In larger communities, outstanding warriors or chieftains were free to focus on military pursuits.

Most of the population would have lived in the lowlands in circular huts, made of wood or stone. Huts like these have been excavated at green Noey and stand rip rig. At Norton on the southwest of Harris, the inhabitance lived in excavated trenches, roofed with hides and timber. In the later Bronze Age many settlements were fortified. At this time there was a change in climate, which likely brought about farming in Highland areas. Cup and ring markings made on Rock Faces and upright stones are circular indentations surrounded by one or more concentric circles. Examples of these markings can be found at temple wood and Achnabrack in Argyle and Balak Mile in Ayrshire.

The burials of the Bronze Age consisted of single grave cremations or inhumanities. Many of these graves are made insists or pits inside of hinges or stone circles, such as the stone circle at color, Lee West Hill. There are also sites like loan head of Deviat inverurie where over 30 cremations were buried in a circular enclosure.

The Iron Age is the time of the Celts who occupied central and Western Europe. The Celts were a very loose confederation of tribes who shared the same language and customs. Around 700 BC the Celts arrived in Britain bringing their language, knowledge of iron smelting and fork Construction. A few groups of Celts may have crossed the North Sea to arrive on the east coast of Scotland, but most are believed to have migrated to Scotland from England. Most of the population farmed the land and lived in round huts with large conical roofs of fache hide or turf supported in the middle by tall posts. In the south of Scotland where wood was plentiful, the dwellings were made of timber or wattle and Daub. Further north walls of the huts were made of stone.

In several parts of Scotland Larders known as sue terrains had been found. These are underground lined with stone, which would have been ideal for preserving food. Among the best examples are Cus, Aboyne and grain and Reno bester on Orkney mainland and castle law near Edinburgh. A small group of huts and a small field were fenced to create a palisaded settlement, which was common in Scotland, such as new and old canard Aboyne. Large settlements also existed such as Tappa North Riney. Where up to at 150 hut platforms have been identified inside the Fort.

Crannogs were settlements on an artificial island made of stone or timber, which were mainly found in central or southern

Scotland. A crannog has been reconstructed at the Scottish Crenoug center on locktay at Kenmore, which is based on the excavated example of Oak Bank locktay. Brocks are fortified circular stone towers that are mainly found in north and west Scotland, like Downtrodden. Glen Aog, Dones or forts are found mainly in the south and east of Scotland and are most often located on hills. One of the largest hill forts is Eildon Hill, Melrose, which had strong ramparts. Both Brocks and hill forts continued to be used after the Iron Age and into the Roman period. Several graves within the ditched area at Karen PayPal Hill, West Lothian are among the few burials identified as being from the Iron Age. Little is known about Iron Age burial.

The Roman Scotts is an Irish Celtic word that means pirate or Raiders, a name given to Raiders from Ireland by the Romans. The Scott's also settled in western Scotland in the fourth and fifth centuries A.D. Another race of people lived in Scotland who was known as the Picts. The Romans referred to all the tribes in Scotland, whether Scott or Picts as Caledonians. The Scotts inhabited Scodia and the Picts Picktavia. The Picts were an amalgam of people who were the original inhabitants of the land and little is known about them. They tattooed their foreheads and other body parts.

The Scotts lived in simply constructed round houses made of wattle and Daub with thatched roofs. They shared rooms with their animals and slept on a lump of Straw. They had wool cloaks made from sheep they kept that shielded them from the frequent rain.

They wore trousers. They had gold and silver broaches for clothes with abstract animal designs, torques, necklace of gold, swords and daggers with jeweled hilts and helmets with bronze and enamel inlay. Those who did not farm were skilled craftsmen, such as blacksmiths, coppersmiths, carpenters, stone masons, potters, weavers, fetcher's and jewelers or merchants. Julius Caesar had invaded Britain in 55 BC and the conquest continued and expanded, but did not reach Scotland.

In A.D 79 the new Roman governor of Britain, Denaze Julius Agricola, sent a fleet to survey Scotland's coast and it was on this excursion that the Romans discovered that Britain was an island. The Celts in Scotland had made some preparations for a Roman attack, but there was no dominant chief or central government. The Celts disliked central organization. The Crannogs, natural or artificial islands used for settlement in Galloway were fortified. New Dones, forts were built and older ones repaired. Some Brocks, circular stone towers in the south were strengthened.

Agricola led legions slowly northward on the first invasion of Scotland. He built roads and fortifications as he pushed further north. The Caledonians led successful guerrilla attacks. Agricola continued his advance until he reached the Caledonian stronghold in the summer of A.D 84, somewhere at a place called Mons Gropius. 30,000 Caledonians faced a Roman force only half their size. However, the untrained half naked natives were no match for the professional Roman army who killed 10,000 Caledonian during the engagement, those who were left fled into the woods. Despite his victory, the emperor Domitian recalled Agricola the following year and did not pursue the campaign. Continued raiding by southern Caledonians prompted the emperor Hadrian to begin construction of a stone wall known as Hadrian's Wall in A.D 122. 20 years later, a lesser structure known as Antonians wall was completed across the narrowest part of Scotland, from the firth of forth to the firth of Clyde.

These walls were more than just fortifications. They were boundaries of the Roman Empire. The last envision of Scotland was orchestrated by Emperor Lucy's Septimius Severus and continued by his son, Kara Kalea. Military basis from this era had been found at South Shields, Kreman and Car pile. They were estuary forts designed to provision large armies by sea. The attempt to subdue Scotland failed and by the end of the second century, the Romans abandoned Scotland. By the fourth century Raiders from Ireland, were carving out territories in southwestern Caledonia and in 4/10 Rome fell.

When the Germanic tribes migrated to Britain after the fall of Roman Britain, they pushed the Celts, who did not want to mingle with the newcomers into Wales and the Kingdom of

Cambria and Strathclyde in southern Scotland. Scotland is made up of four people's, the Picts who were the native population of Scotland. Some scholars believe that they were Celts. Others believe that they migrated from Cynthia, Modern Day Ukraine, and are the ancestors of the city and nomadic horsemen. The Scotts who migrated from Ireland around the sixth century, the Britons, the Celtic tribe that had been Romanized and occupied the territory south of Hadrian's wall and the Angles a German tribe who settled in the east of Scotland.

From 460-490 the legendary author, King of the Britons as claimed to have led a band of elite Celtic warriors against the invading Saxons. The debate about whether King Arthur was real or imagined continues today. Arthur appears in the literature of the later middle Ages. Arthur is said to have fought 12 battles. The main battle being Munns Budonicas. His victory at this battle is said to have held back the Totemic invaders for 40 years. The site of this battle remains unknown.

The two dominant Confederations of tribes that eventually merged to form Scotland were the Picts and the Celts, the Picts ruled Picktavia, also known as Caledonia by the Romans. The Picts were firstly called Caledonian. Later became known as Picts, meaning painted ones, referring to the tattoos they wore. In 600 Picktavia encompassed all of modern day Scotland except for a small kingdom in the southeast known as Dell Riata which was held by the Scotts.

There were northern Picts and southern Picts. Both apparently had sub kings but all Picts were under the rule of one king who ruled all of Picktavia. The Picts and the Scots fought against each other. King Briday of the Picts who died in 584 won a victory against the Gabbrand the king of the Scots. This brought a period of peace between the two peoples. Briday was the first Pictish king to show an interest in Christianity. He was ministered to by Saint Columbia who had arrived from Ireland on the isle of Iona in 565 on the southeast coast of Scotland where he established a monastery. St Columbia is often credited with the conversion of the Scots, but this had occurred prior to his arrival.

In 658 King Osby of North Umbria, one of the seven kingdoms of Anglo Saxon England extended the territory of North Umbria into Picktavia. This territory was held for 30 years and this resulted in close associations between the Picts and North Umbria's. In 685 Briday defeated the North Umbrian's at the battle of Nextel's mirror. The Norwegian Vikings raided Scotland in 787 for the first time. Lindisfarne monastery was destroyed in 793. Iona was raided three times between 795 and 806. By the ninth century the Vikings were seeking new land and were beginning to settle in northern Scotland in the Hebrides, the Orkneys and in the Shetlands. At the same time, they were settling the northeast coast of England. The Vikings intermarried with the Picts and Scots with the intention of conquering all of Scotland.

Kenneth McClain, King of the Scots was threatened by the Vikings as were the Picts. In 836 he received the assistance of Godfrey Mac Fergus, lard of Oreille in Ireland. In fighting against the Vikings. In 839 the Picts suffered a defeat at the hands of the Vikings. Kenneth took advantage of the situation and marched against the Picts and united the two kingdoms in 843. He was the first king of the clans who took the name of their chief. For example, Mac or Mick means son of, so the clan Mac Donald's means son of Donald.

In 934 Athelstan King of all England invaded the Scottish king Constantine the second and defeated him. He recognized Athelstan as is overlord, but in 943 he abdicated his throne and his brother Malcolm the first who took the throne and agreed to accept Edmund the first Afilestand successor as this overlord. In 973 Edgar King of England took a fleet through Scottish waters to frighten Kenneth the second into subservience to England. These events are the basis of England's claim to sovereignty over Scotland. However, in 1018 Malcolm the second king of Scotland fought to Annex Lothian in Roxboro.

In 1034 Duncan the first became king of Scotland. He is the monarch portrayed by Shakespeare in Macbeth. He is the first of the house of Canmore. The Celtic system of succession was known as Tenistry, succession through the male line. No female succession or male succession via female lines was allowed. This led to many successions which resulted in the killing of one's predecessor. Thus dunkin the first was killed by his cousin Macbeth in 1040 and in 1057 Malcolm Kenmore killed Macbeth.

In 1070 William the conqueror extended empire to include Western and northern England. He rappelled the English and bought off Danish forces that were aiding English. The last to resist was Edgar, the Ethylene who fled to King Malcolm of Scotland. Malcolm had married Margaret, Edgar's sister, which allied him with the Anglo Saxons. Much to the displeasure of the Vikings. Traditional allies of the Scots. In 1072 William marched into Scotland to demand that Malcolm stop aiding Edgar. Malcolm agreed and with the piece of Abernethy, Malcolm recognized William as his overlord, who was content to leave Scotland alone as his conquest of England was complete.

In 1092 King Malcolm, the third of Scotland, regained the Scottish lands of Lothian in North Umbria. Rufus established a stronghold at Carlyle on the Scottish border. Rebuffed Malcolm and reestablished the piece of Abernathy in which Malcolm recognized Rufus as his overlord. This was the period in Scotland when feudalism was established first in the lowlands and later in the highlands, which continued to adhere to the clan system of rule Norman's in North Umbria Killed Malcolm. Malcolm's Brother Donald Bayne claimed the throne and resisted the Normans. Rufus supported dunkin the second and then Edgar, two of Malcolm's sons who reigned over Scotland and recognized Rufus as overlord. Henry the first of England remained at peace with Scotland, who King's has recognized him as overlord. Henry married Edith, who took the name Matilda, daughter of Malcolm the third former king of Scotland.

Henry married one of his many illegitimate daughters, Savilla to Alexander, who later became Alexander the first king of Scotland. David, the first 1124 to 1153 is credited with introducing Norman feudalism to Scotland. However, his two predecessors, Edgar and Alexander the first had also done their part to introduce feudalism, but it was David the first who opened the way for feudalism to spread into the lowlands. England's first civil war began when King David the first of Scotland, Matilda's uncle took advantage of the situation and reasserted old territorial claims on border lands including Cambria and Carlyle.

David the first invaded England and was defeated at the battle of the standard in 1138 but gained most of North Umbria not in battle, but as a result of the second treaty of Durham in 1139. David the first continued to establish feudalism in Scotland.

Malcolm the fourth had taken the throne in 1153 just shortly before Henry the second assumed his throne. He was the grandson of King David. His father, Prince Henry had died unexpectedly, leaving Malcolm to assume the throne at the tender age of 12. Malcolm was surrounded by Norman advisers, which prompted two revolts at Moray and Lulac early in his reign. Henry the second assisted with these revolts and took advantage of the situation to press Malcolm the fourth to give up his claim to North Umbria, which he did. Malcolm did not marry or have children and was succeeded by his brother William, who attacked Henry the second in 1173 and 1174 in attempts to regain North Umbria.

He was unsuccessful and was captured during the 1174 attack. Henry the second forced William to swear an oath of allegiance as Henry's feudal superior and had him evacuates forces at several of his castles, which were handed over to English garrisons. Scotland was to benefit from the rule of English King Richard the first. Richard needed money for his crusade and in 1189 he canceled the obligation of the Scottish king to pay homage to England in exchange for 10,000 silver marks. Scotland again became independent and the surrounding castles were returned to their owners. William King of Scott's tried to get his claim to the northern counties recognized before John, as William had tried to do with Richard. William failed a second time. In 1209 John entered a treaty with

William and paid him 15,000 marks for his goodwill. He handed two of his daughters to be married to English princess.

In 1214 his son Alexander the second succeeded William and invaded England in pursuit of the northern counties. He was unsuccessful and John, who was busy with the rebellious barons who would soon force him to sign the Magna Carta was in no position to exact anything from Alexander the second. In 1237 Henry the third King of England came to terms with Alexander the second, king of Scotland, granting him lands in Northumberland and Cumberland. His son Alexander the third succeeded Alexander the Second. Alexander the third successfully defended Scotland from Norwegian Vikings under King Hauntcon who died sailing home from battle. His successor Magnus, surrendered the Western islands to Scotland while the Orkneys and Shetlands remained Norwegian. It was a time of great prosperity in Scotland. The influences that Scotland had felt from the Vikings were gradually changing the economy, from bartering goods to the use of currency.

Boroughs developed, which were small towns surrounded by a rampart and wooden fence. The first borough was Berwick upon tweed, now in England. Others were sterling, Dumbfirline, Perth, scone and Edinburgh. While the highlands still accepted the law of the clan chiefs, the laws of the lowlands were administered through the sheriffs who ruled Shires for the king. The sheriff collected taxes and rents for the king, heard lawsuits, criminal cases, and summoned levies on men when they were needed to bear arms for the King. Alexander the third, the Scottish king had chosen to attend Edwards's coronation. The opportunity for Edward to tightened his grip on Scotland arose when Alexander was unexpectedly killed in a riding accident in 1286, leaving no male heir to the throne. His air was Margaret, a girl of four who was the daughter of Eric of Norway, and his wife Margaret Alexander's daughter. Edward arranged that she be betrothed to the first Prince of Wales. However, the infant Queen Margaret, the made of Norway as she was known, died in 1290 in Orkney on her way to Scotland. The cause of her death is unknown.

Now there were several claimants for the Scottish thrown, the two main ones being John Bailio representing the senior survivor of the House of Canmore and Robert Bruce, who based his claim on being the son of Isabella the second daughter, and had already been recognized as heir. Edward came north to decide which should be king in order to prevent a civil war. Edward at first tried to press a claim that he should be the Scottish king, but he failed to offer a good claim. Edward Chose Bailio and it is often said that he chose Bailio because he would act in Edwards's interest. However Bailio was the choice of the Scottish people. Edward had all claimants pay homage to him prior to the appointment. John Bailio was known as Tomb tabard or empty coat for his weakness in complying with

Edwards demands. The final Straw came in 1294 when Edward was preparing to fight Phillip the fourth of France who had taken possession of Gascony. The last plant [28:54 inaudible] land in France.

Bailio was called to London to supply men to fight in France. The Scottish Bishops Berles and Barons could not endure this, and Bailio did not report to London. Furthermore, he entered into a treaty with France, known as the Halled alliance. Edward viewed this as an act of war and responded in April of 1296 by sending more troops to Scotland than he had sent to whales. The result was that by July, Bailio yielded his crown to Edward. As always, Edward attack the cultural identity of those he conquered. This was done by carrying the stone of scone on which all Scottish kings had been crowned back to Westminster in London. English officials took over the Scottish government.

Now we come to a great Scottish Patriot William Wallace, immortalized by the movie Brave heart, the son of a knight and one of the few Scots who never paid homage to Edward. Wallace led guerrilla attacks in the south with great success. However, William was not alone in the north. Andrew Demori was also leading a guerrilla attacks with even greater success. When Morei March to south and Wallace marched north to meet him at Sterling. They joined forces for a major military attack. On September, 11, 1297 the battle of Sterling Bridge was fought. The Scots won by using a guerrilla tactic of letting the English start crossing a wooden bridge. Then while the English were bottlenecked, the Scots attacked. Morei was fatally wounded and Wallace who had never had the ambition of being Scotland's king was declared guardian of Scotland.

For the next year Wallace issued Ritz and made appointments in the name of the deposed Bailio. On July 22nd, 1298 the inevitable battle between Wallace and Edward took place at Fallkirk. The Scots suffered a slaughter due to the developing technology of the Longbow. English archers cut down the Scots. Had it not been for the English Longbow?

The history of Scotland might have been far different. Wallace survived traveling abroad to France and other countries trying to gain support for the cause of independence in Scotland. Years later in 1305 he was betrayed in Glasgow. He was given a mock trial and suffered a live disownment. Wallace was a Scottish Patriot to the end. Robert, the Bruce had helped in the cause of Scottish independence, but there were times when his political ambition to become king of Scotland led him to avoid conflict. With Wallace gone the Bruce killed his main rival, John Coleman, by stabbing him at the altar at Greyfriars church in Dumfries. Then in 1306 he declared himself king of Scotland. This caused so much division in Scotland that The Bruce had to leave the country for a few months.

Upon his return, he engaged in guerrilla warfare as Wallace had done, The Bruce was said to have observed a spider in a cave reweaving its web against the weather, which is said to have caused him to resolve, to keep up his efforts against England. Edward died while on the march against the Bruce. Edward the second came to the English throne after his father's death. He did not possess the same leadership qualities as Edward the first. Bruce engaged in skirmishes, avoiding pitched battles and possessed a swift moving cavalry. Unlike the heavy, slow moving cavalry of the English. One by one, the English strongholds fell. Forfar, Brechin, Dundee, Perth, Dumfries, Linlithgow, Roxboro, and Edinburgh. Sterling was now the only English held castle in Scotland. This led up to Bruce's famous victory at the battle of Bannockburn where he was greatly outnumbered.

In 1314 Edward the second made a truce with Scotland for 13 years. By that time, Scotland had formally gained her independence. In 1327 Edward the third made an unsuccessful attempt to subdue Scotland, which ended with the treaty of Northampton. Bruce was recognized as king of an independent Scotland and his son was betrothed to Edwards's sister. David the second succeeded his father, Robert the Bruce, but was nothing like him. David almost lost everything during a time when Scotland's resources were depleted by war. What Scotland needed most was peace and time to rebuild. However, David Rashly invaded England, suffering a great defeat and being taken captive from 1346 to 1357. David would have agreed to have had the Scottish crown past to Edward or one of his sons if he died childless. And if parliament had agreed to the proposal, which they rejected. Parliament came to the rescue of Scotland again in 1363 when David agreed to pass the crown to England, if he remained childless. This time parliament had to pay England a ransom to get out of the arrangement. Under David's reign the people of Scotland suffered from increased taxes and the Black Death.

Chapter 3: The Emergence of the Scottish Nation State

The rising presence of foreign influence in the north can be traced back to Malcolm Canmore, who became the king of Alba as Malcolm The third in 1058, after Macbeth's death the previous year. His first wife Ingeborg had been the daughter of a Norse Earl of Orkney, but his second wife Margaret, was a descendant of England's Saxon Royal House. As a queen consort and patroness of the church, Margaret ushered in a climate of receptiveness to southern cultural influences, I. E. The Anglicization of Scotland. By influencing her husband and his court, she advanced the causes of the Gregorian reform, which was mainly preoccupied with the clergy's independence from the state and the conquered English population. Margaret also relocated Benedictine Monks from Canterbury England, to her new foundation at Dumbfermline establishing the precedent for non-Gaelic speaking, clergymen to influence Scottish culture.

During Macbeth's relatively long and peaceful rain, Southerners who were loyal to him migrated northwards opting to resettle in the south west and northeast of modern day Scotland. They brought with them a more international outlook and culture, sowing the seeds of foreign influence in predominantly Gaelic society. Gaelic traditions and customs prevailed in everyday life, the church and the Royal Courts as well as the institutions of law and education. This was set to change throughout the 11th and 12th centuries. When Malcolm the third died during his final English raid in 1093 however, there were concerted attempts to prevent the replacement of Tenistry with Primogeniture. This southern custom privileged, the legitimate firstborn son above everyone else. Younger brothers, older or younger, illegitimate sons and collateral relatives when it came to inheriting his parents throne, his State or wealth. Under Tenistry the heir to the king could be the eldest son, but this was not necessarily the case.

A council of family heads could opt to elect a brother, nephew, or cousin of the previous chieftain. Anyone who is linked by blood and deemed most worthy of the position. Malcolm the thirds, brother and son from his first marriage, each briefly occupied the throne after his death. In time however, it was Malcolm the thirds three sons with the assistance of Margaret who secured their control over the throne. Edgar was king from 1097 to 1107, followed by Alexander the first 1107 to 1124 and David the first 1124 to 1153. With the help of the English they defied Celtic opposition and claims from the descendants of their father's first marriage. Their rise to power was accompanied by the increasing practice of Primogeniture, which finally replaced Tenistry permanently during the late 13th century. The presence of Latin in Scotland had linked it to the international culture of the Christian Church over the previous decades, which paved the way for the impact of other influences from continental Europe.

Throughout the 12th and 13th centuries the Europeanization of Europe was underway, as the modern western European state began developing in England, France, Norway, and Germany. They were categorized by clearly defined borders, national sovereignty, a commercial economy, parliamentary representation, thoroughly institutionalized administrative and legal systems, and a shared idea of nationhood. The arrival of immigrants from Normandy, Brittany and Flanders accelerated the disruption of Gaelic norms and traditions, ringing in new influences, ideas and practices that could be repurposed for Scottish ends. David the first, the youngest of Malcolm the thirds six sons with Margaret, played a major role in Scotland's evolution into a modern nation state. He eventually proved himself to be one of the most powerful and influential Scottish kings. Unlike his mother, who did not interfere much with the inner workings of the church. He actively reorganized Scottish Christianity to align it with its counterparts in England and continental Europe. This meant that there was a clear division between the secular and regular clergy, as well as a complete system of parishes and diocese.

He also founded several religious communities, mainly for Cistercian Monks and Augustinian cannons. On the political front, David the first introduced an Anglo French Norman aristocracy that would go on to play a significant role in Scottish history. Much of his early life had been spent at the court of his brother-in-law, King Henry the first of England, like his father before him, his marriage to a prominent English woman, a daughter of Walty of Earl of North Umbria, earned him significant political clout in England. Through his wife, he became the Earl of Huntington, a title that came with large swathes of land in Northampton shire. His Anglo Norman connections helped him secure the right to rule Cambria, Strathclyde and part of Lothian before he succeeded the throne from his older brother Alexander the first. Despite his English connections, David the first remained an independent king who was intent on drawing from English, culture and bureaucracy to empower Scotland.

He paved the way for the arrival of other Anglo Norman Families to migrate northward by providing generous rewards of offices and lands. These included Debruises in Annandale, the Fitsilence in Erindale and the Demoravilles in Ayrshire. They were given control of large estates in peripheral areas where David the first regal authority could not be easily enforced. This decentralized form of government, thus introduced a form of feudalism in Scotland. A four tier hierarchy developed with the king at the apex, followed by the Nobles, kings and surfs. The nobles possessed Lens from the crown for their military services, which were provided through the training and recruitment of knights. These knights also protected the peasants on their lords lands who provided their labor and a share of their crops in exchange for this protection. Similar feudal arrangements had existed amongst the clan systems of the Scottish highlands, but these were mainly based on family bonds instead of written charters and legal contracts.

David the first rule over the Scottish kingdom was also consolidated through the creation of a more sophisticated government administration. He introduced the office of Sheriff, vice cops, a royal judge, and an administrator for each area of the kingdom, who was based within a royal castle. Central government officials such as the chancellor, the Chamberlain, and the just sure were introduced to the royal court. The royal court began playing the role of Supreme Court of law and parliament, maintaining an efficient government that facilitated piece and the flourishing of a medieval economy and society. There are four main characteristics which clearly differentiated David the first kingship from the traditional Celtic style kingship that his predecessors had practiced. Firstly, he extended royal power into practically every aspect of life, mainly the religious and the economic. He reformed the Scottish church and extended its religious orders across the land while also introducing an English type market economy.

This included the introduction of formal markets and fairs that required trading licenses that were administered by the crown. He minted the first Scottish coinage and founded the kingdoms four royal burrows, Berwick, Edinburgh, Perth, and Aberdeen. His trusted nobles established firm local lordships centered on well-defended castles. They also sent their nights to serve in his army, which allowed him to experiment with the various tools and policies of an English style administrative kingship. Secondly, he established a more totalizing and monopolistic royal lordship across a greater Scotland, a tradition that greatly benefited his successors. The older tradition of Tenistry, which nearly always engendered great chaos and uncertainty, was abandoned in favor of a strict order for royal succession. This left the regional kings with little opportunity to compete for the throne. Succession was now a matter of direct lineage. True to his centralizing ambitions. David preemptively elected his only son Henry as a co ruler in 1135. After Henry's unexpected early demise in 1152 David appointed his oldest grandson, as is apparent heir.

Malcolm the forth thus became king in 1153 at the previously implausible age of 12 when his grandfather died, a regent nevertheless safeguarded the throne until he was old enough to rule on his own. A strict adherence to primogeniture thus helped to spare the Scottish kingdom from disruptive upheavals and violent competition for the throne. Thirdly, David the first and his government sought to empower the Scottish kingship to be on equal footing with the English kingship. The objective was to thwart to the English monarchies, imperial aspirations, and to foster a greater sense of identity and status as a decidedly independent kingdom. The Scottish Church thus lobbied the pope for PayPal approval of the Scottish kingship. An effort that was thwarted until 1329 by rigorous English lobbying. This concept of a divine and semi sacred kingship was also a potent means for David the first to consolidate his rule.

In the meantime, the Scottish church insisted on remaining independent from the influence of its counterparts in Canterbury or York.

Finally, the Scottish King's began to seek a stronger footing on an international stage. They embraced European courtly fashions and began participating in international diplomacy. David the first succeeded in winning respect and admiration from his continental European peers. The first Scottish monarch to do so. He even envisioned himself as a potential leader of the second crusade. His court embraced English and French, which were both Delingua Franca of political society to such an extent that an Englishman commented that the Scots regarded themselves as Frenchmen in race, manners, language, and culture. Scottish princesses began marrying continental princes with greater frequency while their male counterparts married English, French, and Norwegian princesses, or high born women. From here on the Scottish King's insisted on being viewed as equals to the western European monarchs.

Chapter 4: The Wars of Independence

As in Wales, resistance to Edward the first had led to conquest and direct English rule. But unlike the Welsh, the Scots had not faced heavy losses in their defeat. Even the Battle of Dunbar was not a large engagement, and though it was demoralizing, it did little long term damage to Scotland's military resources. The country might look beaten, but many Scots didn't yet feel that way. Moreover, once he conquered the Scots, Edward the first returned south, the Scottish campaign had drawn time and resources away from his war with the French, and he was determined to waste no more time. However, without the English King keeping them beneath his boot heel. And with much of his armed might draw away to another war, the Scots found the will to resist.

Locked away in England, John Balliol was in no place to lead a fight back against the English, but he remained a figurehead to rally behind and the Scots nobility began appointing sheriffs and other officials in his name, establishing their own resistance government. While a new government and administration was being pulled together, armed forces were being recruited to throw off the English yoke. This took place on three different fronts under different leaders. It had the most politically prominent and therefore legitimate leadership in the southwest, where a group of important lords and churchmen started gathering troops. Among them was Robert the Bruce, a grandson of the contender for the throne, who would also eventually make his reputation fighting the English. In the Northeast Andrew Murray, having escaped English imprisonment after Dunbar led the fight. Between them in the center of the country, forces were gathered by the man who became the most famous leader of this period, William Wallace.

Contrary to popular myth, Wallace was not a peasant or common man an obscure member of a minor noble family. His social status was always likely to lead him to the life of a man at arms, the battlefield role of the upper classes. He had deeper Scottish connections than the more prominent nobles. Having been raised speaking Scots in a Scottish community, rather than in the French speaking cross border Anglo Scottish upper nobility. Still, Wallace would likely have remained an obscure figure long forgotten by history, if not for his loyal adherence to the Balliol cause. Even in Scotland's Darkest Hour, he stood by the absent King rallying armed forces in support of his claim to the throne. Whatever mixture of charisma and local influence allowed him to do it, Wallace gathered troops around him and led a series of successful hit and run raids against the occupiers. His adherence was vital to keeping the Bailio cause alive but that cause was also vital to him and provided a status he would otherwise have lacked.

As the flames of revolt spread across Scotland. Wallace entered the fray, and though hard facts about his initial war efforts are difficult to source. What is clear is that he emerged from obscurity in May 1297 by murdering the English Sheriff of Lanark, William Dehesslerig. Hesslerig was part of the English administration Edward had imposed on Scotland following his conquest the previous year. And at the head of this administration was John de Warren, sixth Earl of Surrey, who had been Edwards chief Lieutenant during the Battle of Dunbar. Assisting Warren was Hugh of Cresingham, who served as treasurer. Wallace's slaying of Hesslerig in May marked an important turning point in the unrest as what had previously been destroyed resistance turned into full blown rebellion. As Sheriff Hesslerig was a symbol of the repressive English authority. And at the time of his murder, he was in Lanark to hold an [04:11 inaudible], a court session for the trial of civil or criminal cases. It would seem that Wallace chose his target in the occasion carefully as the murder of an English official while he was exercising the Kings legal authority over the Scots, would have sent a powerful message to both the occupiers and the occupied. Precisely what Wallace was doing in Lanark in central Scotland in May 1297 is unknown, but popular tradition claims he was there to seek personal revenge against Hesslerig.

The legend stemming from blind Harry's account of Wallace holds that Hesslerig had murdered Wallace's beloved Marion Braid foot. The Eris of Leamington, a village not far from Lanark. It is not clear whether braid foot was Wallace's wife or Mistress but most historians treat the story of Wallace's hot blooded, vengeful murder of Hesslerig as myth and Marion Braid foot as part of this legend, since no evidence supports the personal vengeance claim. It is far more likely than Wallace's brutal murder of Hesslerig was intended to send a chilling message to the English that no one, not even officials would be spared in the mounting rebellion. The English declared Wallace an outlaw, but many Scots were inspired by his actions and joined his campaign. Immediately after Lanark Wallace's forces grew, spurred on perhaps by the rumor that Edward was looking to suppress Midland Scotland in order to force the men of that region into his army to fight against France.

In August 1297, Edward the first headed off to fight in Flanders, leaving Surrey and his associates to deal with the supposedly beaten Scots. He could not afford to abandon his adherents north of the border to the rebels, or allow his recent conquest to be undone. But he also could not abandon his existing plans against the French to deal with the growing revolt, as this would make the rebels look more credible. Thus he left the war to his lieutenants this time, confident that they could crush the Scots without him. In June 1297, the English led by Henry Percy and Robert Clifford, crossed into Annandale from Cumberland and burnt lock maiden on their way to Irvine. A Scottish army under the leadership of Douglas Robert Wishart, the Bishop of Glasgow, James Stewart, one of the former guardians of Scotland, and a recent convert to the patriotic cause Robert the Bruce gathered to face the English threat. Not long after the English cavalry advanced against them. The Scots sought to negotiate terms of surrender, but the negotiations were unusually lengthy. A fact that has led some historians to argue that the negotiated surrender was merely a ruse to give Wallace more time to assemble an army.

Cresingham Edwards's treasure distrusted the Scots and raised an army to fight Wallace. But he was stopped by Percy and Clifford, who believed they had successfully pacified Scotland south of Lanark. As it turned out, the English military leaders had underestimated their opponents. Following the capitulation at Irvine in July 1297, the Scots failed to surrender the hostages they had promised the English and Stewart and Bruce rejoined the Scottish forces only a short time later.

Wallace had since left the forest of Selkirk to head north, where according to blind Harry, he burned 100 English ships. Historian Andrew Fisher believes that was more likely the work of Andrew Murray. But either way, Wallace went on to push out the English from Fife and Perthsure.

By August he was laying siege to Dundee. And according to the chronicler Walter of Guisborough Wallace had attained a large and diverse following. The common folk of the land followed Him as their leader and ruler, the retainers of the great Lords adhere to him. And even though the Lords themselves were present with the English king in body at heart, they were on the opposite side. By uniting their forces in a single army, Murray and Wallace signal to the world that they believe they could beat the odds that in the right circumstances, and with the right leadership, they could defeat the English in a pitched battle, striking a decisive blow for Scottish freedom. The authority King Edward had reclaimed over Scotland the previous year was all but gone by the late summer of 1297. At the time, his Cresingham sent to his monarch the following assessment of the situation. By far the greater part of your counties of the realm of Scotland is still un-provided with keepers. Some have given up their bailiwicks and others neither will nor dare return.

And in some counties the Scots have established and place the bailiffs and ministers so that no counties in proper order, excepting Berwick and Rocks Borough and this only lately. Finally acknowledging that the Scottish rebellion was strong and growing, the English at last aimed to take firm action. Warren Edwards chief Lieutenant, who had succeeded at Dunbar in 1296 left Berwick and headed for Sterling with a sizable army, accompanied by Cresingham they, arrived near Sterling in early September. Meanwhile, Wallace left the siege of the castle at Dundee to the town's inhabitants, and also headed to Sterling. Having joined forces with Andrew Murray, whose successful rebellion in the north of Scotland had severely weakened the English there. Together the two headed what the English called a very large body of rogues. And in early September, they took up positions on the southward looking slope of the abbey Craig, about a mile north of a narrow wooden bridge stretching across the river forth. This bridge situated near Sterling castle was highly strategic because the river was too deep and wide to cross below Sterling, and to the West Lake Flanders moss, Marsh land that was impossible to cross with an army. Furthermore, Sterling Bridge tied the north and south of Scotland together. So whoever controlled this site would hold a strategic advantage over the opponent.

Wallace and Murray even with their entire Scottish army in the field, were about to face a test of strength. The English army with its heavy cavalry outnumbers the Scots by a comfortable margin. A fact that might have caused Warren to expect another easy victory like at Dunbar. He and Cresingham also had the advantage of experience on their side. Since neither Wallace nor Murray could claim extensive military practice, and neither had ever before commanded a large force. However, despite these clear advantages, Warren did not seem bent on engaging in battle. In the days before the battle, he sent representatives to negotiate the surrender of the Scots and when that failed, he sent two Dominican friars, as envoys to speak with Wallace and Murray in order to procure from them terms of surrender. Much to Warren's surprise, he received in response, not a capitulation. But Wallace is well known rebuff. Go back and tell your people that we have not come here for peace. We are ready rather to fight to avenge ourselves and to free our country. Let them come up to us as soon as they like, and they will find us prepared to prove the same in their beards. Hearing Wallace's slight Warren ordered an attack.

Earlier on the morning of September 11, 1297 the English army led by Cresingham began to cross a sterling bridge at a painstakingly slow pace, as the bridge was wide enough for only two horsemen to stand abreast. However, even after some 5000 made it across, Warren, who had overslept that morning and arrived late to the site, promptly recalled all of them. Warren convened a council of war, but he ignored the wise advice of a former Scottish Knight, Richard Lundy, who had suggested crossing the river with his cavalry at a nearby Ford were 60 horsemen could traverse together in order to outflank the Scots. Cresingham preferred the bridge crossing and Warren differed to his opinion. As a result, the army again began a slow crossing of the bridge. Wallace and Marie observed the enemy's maneuvers from the abbey Craig and waited until a certain number of the enemy had reached their side of the river. Once satisfied, they ordered their infantry down the slope along the narrow Causeway to the bridge.

The English cavalry whose horses were unable to gain solid ground on the marshy terrain floundered as the Scots seized the northern end of the bridge, there by cutting off the advancing force from the rest of the army and from the hope of reinforcements. While the rest of the English army watched, the Scots annihilated or let drown some 5000 infantry and 100 knights, including Cresingham, whose body was flayed and made into trophies. Tradition holds that Cresingham skin was used to make Wallace's sword belt. The Lennar coast Chronicle reported that Wallace had a broad strip taken from the head to the heel, to make a baldric for his sword. While Cresingham and the men on the other side of the bridge suffered their grisly fates, Warren never crossed the bridge. As he witnessed the slaughter of his men from afar. He now had to worry about preventing the Scots from crossing the river in pursuit of what remained of the English army. So Warren ordered the bridges destruction and then promptly fled back to Berwick.

Naturally, the battle is best remembered for the way in which blind Harry described it, even as his fantastical account is filled with inaccuracies. On Saturday, they Murray and Wallace Road onto the bridge, which was a good plane board well-made and jointed, having placed watches to see that none past from the army. Taking a right the most able workmen there, he Wallace ordered him to saw the plank in two at the mid straight, middle stretch, so that no one might walk over it. He then nailed it up quickly with hinges and dirtied it with clay to cause it to appear that nothing had been done. The other end he so arranged that it would lie on three wooden rollers which were so placed that when one was out, the rest would fall down. The right himself, he ordered to sit there underneath in a cradle bound on a beam to lose the pin when Wallace let him know, by blowing a horn when the time came. No one in all the army should be allowed to blow but he, the day of the great battle approached. For power the English would not fail. They were ever six to one against Wallace. 50,000 made for the place of battle. The remainder abiding at the castle, both field and Castle they thoughts to conquer at their will.

The worthy the Scots upon the other side of the river took the Plainfield on foot. Hugh Cresingham leads on the Vanguard with 20,000 likely men to sea. 30,000 the Earl of Warren had, but he did then as wisdom did direct. All the first army being sent over before him. Some Scottish men, who well knew this manner of attack Bade Wallace sound, saying they were now enough, then the remainder fled, not able to abide longer, seeking suckler in many directions, some East, some West and some fled to the North. 7000 full at once floated in the fourth, plunged into the deep and drowned without mercy. None were left alive of all that fell army.

Regardless of the subsequent embellishments, Wallace and Marie's achievement at Sterling Bridge was nothing less than remarkable. Despite their inferior numbers, and an army composed of a ragtag host of peasants, farmers and Burgess's, the two leaders exploited the terrain and outwitted and outmaneuver the far more experienced Warren and his heavy cavalry. The effects of this resoundingly victory were felt immediately too. Dundee and Sterling's castles surrendered. While the town's Edinburgh and Berwick also fell to the Scots, though their castles remained in English hands. When the towns of Headington and Rocks Borough were burnt. English hold over Scotland had been all but eliminated.

While the victory at Sterling Bridge decisively swung the wars momentum behind the Scots. It came at a cost. Andrew Murray was grievously injured during the battle and died in early November. Despite his injuries over the two months between Sterling Bridge and his death, Marie and Wallace work together as leaders not only of the Scottish army, but of the country as a whole. In October, the two sent Mrs. to the mayors and communes of Hamburg, and Lubec in an attempt to restore trading relations with Germany. And in early November, Wallace followed up this attempt at diplomacy by securing the election of William Lumberton, who turned out to be staunchly anti-English, as the Bishop of St Andrews. Around that time, Murray passed away from the wounds he had sustained at Sterling Bridge, leaving the burden of defending Scotland solely on Wallace's shoulders.

For the next year, Wallace would hold the highest rank of power and authority in Scotland. The Scottish victory at Sterling bridge came as a huge shock to the English and doubtless to summon Scotland as well. With Surrey defeated and his army in tatters Men all across Scotland joined the rebel cause. Nobles who had previously sworn fealty to Edward turned coat and raised bands of soldiers to fight against him. With momentum on his side, Wallace went on the offensive against England, and by the end of October 1297, he had invaded English territory by marching his growing army into Northumberland and taking its inhabitants by surprise. From Northumberland Wallace led his men across the northwest of England, arriving as far as Cocermouth. While it sounds particularly bold, Wallace was at least partly forced to march into England, because Scotland was stricken by famine and his army which had grown markedly in size needed more resources. It was during this period that Wallace earned the reputation among the English as a ruthless and violent brute.

Without siege machines, the Scottish army could not take any English cities of consequence, so they resorted to raiding and pillaging less protected towns. According to Walter of Guisborough, the services of God totally ceased in all the monasteries and churches between Newcastle and Carlisle. For all the cannons, monks and priests fled before the face of the Scots as did nearly all the people. The reputation for ferocity and barbarity that Wallace had gained at this time, remained with him for centuries after his death, even though as Andrew Fisher claims the cruel acts he ordered were, like those ordered by Edward the first at Berwick, and were of a kind often repeated by both sides. By late November after a failed attempt to raid the bishop brick of Durham, the severe weather forced the end of the invasion of England. Wallace and his troops returned north. Using his title of guardian of the realm. Wallace tried to reestablish order in Scotland in the name of john the first. But despite a growing mass of popular support, he was undermined by a lack of support from the nobility.

Many Scottish nobles resented Wallace's quick rise to power. And according to some contemporaries, Wallace didn't hesitate to use harsh measures against his detractors at home. Stories of imprisonment and hangings made the rounds in both Scotland and England, confirming in the eyes of the English Wallace's status as a violent Biggent. In fact, it was a shared sentiment that Wallace should be defeated that brought the English people together in support of their monarchs renewed campaign in Scotland. In the winter of 1297 to 1298. Edward had been in Flanders overseen his campaign against France, and he did not return to England until my march 1298 after a truce was negotiated with the French. Almost immediately, he said about preparing for war with the Scots and even transferred the seat of government north to York in order to be closer to his target. In April, he convened a war Council in York to plan a campaign, but the Scottish magnates ordered to attend ignored his directive. In retaliation, Edward announced the forfeiture of their lands.

On June 25, the king's army assembled at Rocks Borough, and Edward joined them by early July. Edward headed a strong force composed of roughly 2000 to 3000 horseman, and about 14,000 infantry, many of whom were Welsh, but as he led the army north and advanced into Scotland through Lauderdale, he found the land devastated and empty of inhabitants, which deprived him of the opportunity to gain intelligence about the Scottish army's whereabouts. While Edwards's preparations for war are well known, Wallace's own actions during this time are far less understood. In fact, it is impossible to place in between his return to Scotland in November 1297, following the raid of Northern England and March 1298, when documents show his presence at Porfican in Linlithgowsure on March 29. However, these documents also revealed that by March 1298, Wallace had two new titles, knight and guardian of the kingdom, both in addition to his already established role as leader of the army.

He was the first Scott to be the sole holder of the second title, guardian of the kingdom. The dates he received those titles are unknown, but it's safe to assume the military prowess he exhibited throughout 1297 was the reason they were bestowed on him. Of course, to Edward Wallace's titles meant nothing.

By the summer of 1298 Edwards's sole aim was to locate and subsequently annihilate Sir William and his motley army. But Wallace was not eager to engage in battle with the English and thus engaged in a shrewd strategy of withdraw, heading ever farther north and leaving nothing but scorched earth behind him. Edward took the bait and continued advancing deeper into Scotland, overstretching his lines of communication and supplies just as well as had hoped. Unable to locate the enemy or live off the land. His army was soon starving and in disarray. On July 19, when the army was at Temple Liston, a large supply of wine reaches them, and Edward promptly distributed it. The Welsh soldiers became drunk and ended up rioting, killing several priests. Edward unleashed his cavalry on them and at 80 Welsh soldiers were killed. Many others threatened to change sides before the outbreak was finally quelled. Following this clash, Edward decided to retire to Edinburgh. Wallace's strategy was working, and he was yet again outwitting King Edward. Edward was on the verge of retreat, when fortune finally smiled on him on July 21.

Two Earls had a messenger convey intelligence to the king, that Wallace and his men were stationed at Fall Kirk, less than 20 miles away. The messenger also informed Edward of Wallace's intention to attack the retreating English army by night. Edward acted at once and immediately directed his army toward fall Kirk. That night they camped near the Scottish forces, and the king ordered his men to sleep with their horses beside them in case the Scots attacked. Chaos soon ensued when Edward himself was injured by his horse and the soldiers panicked, and it was only by mounting his horse to display his strength that the king was able to calm his men. At sunrise The next morning, he led his army toward Fall Kirk. Edward came upon Wallace in a strongly entrenched position, protected by a morass which was hidden from the English. Though Wallace had attempted to avoid battle, he at least found himself in a strong position when Edward surprised him with his men arranged to fight.

When the English spotted them, the Scots were divided into four shield drums. The core Scottish battle strategy. A shield drum, was the formation of as many as 2000 men brandishing 12 foot long spears, and gathered in either huge circles or rectangles to look something like a lethal hedgehog. The ranks of the shield drum were to be packed tightly to be nearly impenetrable. With this formation, the Scottish infantry could face off against mounted cavalry men, England's strongest weapon. Between the shield drums Wallace had station his archers, and behind everyone stood the modest side Scottish cavalry under the command of John Commen. Despite having a clear advantage, as well as the benefit of the element of surprise, Edward preferred not to engage immediately and instructed his army to rest. However, several men, including the Earls of Norfolk, Hereford and Lincoln, refused to follow his order and lead a unit forward toward the Scots. They were blocked from advancing further by the morass, and had to shift westward splitting into two wings. Once passed the marshland, the English Vanguard clashed with the shield drums, which held their positions and managed to inflict heavy damage on the English cavalry.

In response, Edward called up his archers to weaken the Scottish ranks. When Edward called up the archers, the Scottish cavalry fled, leaving the shield drums and the Scottish archers with no rear support. But even with a barrage of arrows falling on them, the shield drums managed to keep their discipline while they were suffering heavy losses. They also killed more than 100 English horsemen. But Wallace was severely weakened without his cavalry, which became even more evident once Edward withdrew his cavalry and advanced his long Bowman and cross Bowman. The Scottish infantry was massacred by both the hail of arrows and a series of renewed cavalry assaults. Wallace left the field with a small force before the battle was over. But while the English charged him with cowardice, he was apparently working to ensure the escape of

Scottish survivors, many of whom fled into the nearby woods. Wallace headed towards Sterling and burnt the town and the castle once he arrived. Though Edward had wanted Fall Kirk, his army was too depleted to carry on the campaign or to pursue Wallace. So he began to withdraw his troops and was back in Carlisle by September 9. With that, Edwards fight for Scotland was temporarily suspended and the same could be said for Wallace.

Sometime between the Battle of Fall Kirk and the following December, Wallace resigned the guardianship, which was taken over by Robert the Bruce and john Coleman. He traveled to the European continent, where he presented Scotland's case of freedom to various courts. As it turned out, diplomacy proved to be nearly as dangerous as warfare. It is difficult to know for certain where Wallace went first, and some believe he visited Norway before arriving in France in early November 1299, to lobby for King Philip the fourth support. What is clear, though, is that rather than listening to Wallace's case, Philip had him arrested and offered to hand him over to the English. The cause of the king's sudden loyalty to the English his former enemies was Edwards's marriage to his sister Margaret only two months earlier. However, when Edward learned that Wallace was in French captivity, he responded with a surprising lack of interest and urgency. He Merely thanked Philip and requested that he keep Wallace in France until further notice.

There's no clear explanation for Edwards apparent apathy, and speculation suggests that the English King was not bent on Wallace's destruction. Perhaps he considered the Scots to removed and far from the Scottish cause and thus no longer a real threat. But whatever Edwards thinking he made absolutely no attempt to have Wallace brought to England for justice. After a year of watching over Wallace, Philip grew fond of him and released him to carry on his diplomatic campaigns elsewhere. Though Edward had broken the Scottish army, the result was not the total conquest he hoped for. Political opposition from a group of English magnates forced him to withdraw from the job half done. The English now controlled large swathes of Scotland mostly centered on castles in the south and east. But just like the Scottish kings before them, they had a harder time controlling the highlands and Ireland. Scotland was conquered in theory, but the flames of rebellion burned on.

Wallace's army was broken, and with it any claim he had to political authority. In his place, the Scots appointed a pair of Guardians, Robert the Bruce and John Coleman, Lord of Badenoch, who had supported Bailio in the disputed succession. William Lumberton, the Bishop of St. Andrews, was later added as a third guardian to mediate between the two men who seldom saw eye to eye. Under this new leadership, the Scots returned to a strategy of raids and ambushes, rather than trying to engage the English in a pitched battle. There followed several years of small struggles and minor engagements, in which the future of Scotland remained uncertain. In England, the elderly Edward was facing a range of political challenges. Asking for money to fund his wars always created some resistance from the nobles and clergy on whom the burden of payment mostly rested. And Edwards authoritarian leadership style was also leading to some resentment and calls for the reassertion of noble rights.

Like many English monarchs, he had troubles with senior clergyman, the English church and its priests might owe some allegiance as Englishman to the king. But they also owed allegiances to the Pope, and had a duty to defend the church against royal encroachments. Churchmen sometimes resisted Edwards's demands of Taxis or appointed priests to new positions in line with people rather than royal policy. When Archbishop Corbridge of York did this in 1304, it led to an angry confrontation. The king letting no man put a foreign Pope ahead of him. Arguments with the church subsided with political changes in Europe, and the appointment of the pro English Pope Clements the fifth in 1305. But the conflict between how churchmen saw their loyalties and how their monarchs did would remain a constant throughout the Middle Ages. The greatest source of conflict between Edward and the papacy became Scotland. Pressure from the French led him to release the deposed John Bailio into the Pope's custody in 1299. But this was not the end of church intervention.

The papa bull Shemosfely condemned the English occupation of Scotland, and demanded that the English withdraw, a demand that Edward completely ignored. While Edward was occupied with affairs at home, the Scots blockaded Sterling castle, forcing the English Garrison's to surrender after they ran out of food. In May 1300, Edward launched yet another campaign in Scotland to bring the country under his permanent control. He focused in particular on securing the castles and after invading Galloway, he laid siege to Carelaborock castle, near the southern coast of Dumfries. Siege engines were transferred from Lock Maven and surrounding castles in order to force out the 60 Scott's trying to defend the stronghold against the much larger English army. And once Edward finally broke through the defenses, he hanged several of the Scottish fighters from the castles battlements.

However, aside from a few other minor skirmishes, the English campaign of 1300 achieved little else of significance besides rebuke from outsiders. That August the Papacy sent a letter imploring Edward to withdraw from Scotland. Over the spring and summer of the next four years 1301 to 1304. Edward continued to lead campaigns north into Scotland, with the view of bringing the territory definitively under his control. And in 1302, his authority increased when Robert the Bruce submitted to him. Later the same year, even the papacy softened its stance on his place in Scottish affairs as Pope Boniface, the eighth wrote to the Scottish bishops, encouraging them to reconcile with Edward. As his hold over Scotland grew more secure Edward resurrected old practices, such as demanding that the Scottish nobles pay homage to him. He also reestablished an English administration, including English sheriff's in all strategic localities to run several aspects of Scotland's political and legal systems.

During Edwards operations in 1303 however, he experienced difficulties early on due to sustained opposition posed by Wallace, who repeatedly hindered both divisions of the English army from advancing. The king and his men eventually made his way across most of Scotland, before settling for the winter near Dumbfirline, and by early 1304 the tides turned in Edwards favor. On February nine, John Coleman submitted to him, followed by all of the leading and influential Scots except Wallace and a few others. Perhaps one of the reasons Wallace didn't submit is because it wasn't a palatable option. Had Wallace chosen to submit to Edward, he would not have enjoyed the same lenient terms granted to both Bruce and Coleman, because Edward all but excluded him from this option. As for Sir William Wallace, it is agreed that he may render himself up to the will and mercy of our sovereign Lord the king, if it shall seem good to him. In other words, if Wallace surrendered, no clemency was guaranteed.

The invasion of 1303 to 1304 was to be Edward the first last successful act of conquest. Now in his 60s, he was very old by the standards of the time, but still determined to lead his forces in the field, marching in strength through Dundee, Brechin and Aberdeen, the English drove into the heartland of Scotland, proving the inability of the Scots to hold against a large English force. Having advanced as far north as Murray, they returned to Dumbfirline for the winter. Coleman as guardian of Scotland could not muster enough forces to match them. In January 1304, the Scottish nobility, led by Coleman surrendered to Edward. As part of the surrender, Edward agreed that the country's laws and the rights of the nobles would be as they had been under King Alexander. This was a very different surrender from the one that had come before. Edward was diplomatic rather than menacing, returning lands to the Lords who surrender to his rule, and agreeing to the formation of a new committee of both English and Scottish members who would decide how Scotland would be governed. Perhaps having learned a lesson from responses to his previous harshness, or perhaps seeing that his son would need a different approach to keep the Scots in line. Edward used the carrat as well as the stick. With nearly all of the powerful Scott's in his back pocket and Sterling castle now in his possession, Edward intensified his efforts to capture the elusive Wallace.

In March 1304 he had sent a large force, which included Robert the Bruce to fight against the Scottish hero, but it failed to capture him. Pope Boniface the eighth, who had fallen out with Philip the fourth of France, and now needed the English kings backing supported Edwards's occupation. He ordered the Scottish bishops, many of whom had been among the Lord's leading the revolt, to join in obedience to the conquering king. The last bastion of Scottish resistance was at Sterling castle, where the garrison refused to accept the new order. From April to July 1304 Edward laid siege to the castle. In one of the most spectacular pieces of showboating in medieval warfare. Gunpowder a rarity at the time was used to make Greek fire. Massive siege machines were ordered, including the colossal tribute shih war Wolf, a masterpiece of the siege engineer's art that earned its creator Thomas Greenfield the substantial sum of 40 pounds.

A viewing gallery was constructed so that ladies of the English court could watch the siege as it played out. The English combined bombardment with cutting off Scottish supply lines, leaving the castles garrison starving and shaken. Always looking to lead from the front. Edward took part in the siege, and his life was twice put in jeopardy. Once when a crossbow bolt pierced his clothes, and once when a stone from a manganell scared his horse into throwing him. Gray haired but still determined, the aging King responded to the locals resistance by having the lead stripped from church roofs for the counterweights of his siege machines. Short of supplies and without hope of relief the Sterling garrison eventually asked to surrender. Edward did not allow them to do so until war wolf had been completed and tested against their walls. That done and despite earlier threats, he let the 30 men of the garrison leave with their lives. Only their leader Sir William Olyphant was sent to the Tower of London, and only an Englishman who had given the castle to the Scots was executed.

During a skirmish in September 1304 Wallace again managed to escape the English army, but only after inflicting considerable casualties on the army. In response, Edward increased the stakes with bribery and coercion by promising several Scots who had submitted to him, including Coleman to commute their sentences of exile in return for Wallace's capture. Despite the intense pressure on Wallace, it would take Edward nearly another full year to find and detain him. How he lived at large until then, is unknown. As no documents make reference to his movements or actions. But on August 3, 1305 Edward finally got his wish when Wallace was taken by one of his fellow Scots John Menteith, the keeper of Dumbarton castle. Menteith was rewarded with land for his compliance. Edward refused to meet with Wallace following his arrest, and they had him transported to London on August 22. In the early morning of the next day, Wallace arrived and was taken on horseback in a procession of judicial and legal authorities to Westminster Hall. There was frenzy of excitement on the streets, as many Londoners came out to catch a glimpse of the notorious Scottish warrior.

Inside the hall Wallace was accompanied onto a scaffold, where officials placed a laurel crown on his head, in an apparent attempt to humiliate him by deeming him merely a king of outlaws, and it was the only crown they believed he merited. The Justice presiding over the trial presented the indictment, accusing Wallace of treason and engaging in war crimes by spearing neither age nor sex, monk nor nun. While admitting to the other allegations, Wallace denied the charges of treason, replying, I could not be a trader to Edward, for I was never his subject. No examination of evidence took place, nor was any testimony of witnesses heard. Wallace was not permitted to defend himself because his legal status was that of an outlawed thief. Obviously, the proceedings were a mere formality, and the judgment was given on the same day, William Wallace was found guilty of treason against the English King for taking up arms against him in Scotland, and for making an alliance with France, and he received the standard sentence for treason.

He was to be drawn to the gallows on a hurdle by horses through the streets of London, where he would be hanged for the crimes of murder and robbery. As a desecrater of churches he was to be cut down from the gallows while not quite dead, in order that his internal organs and genitals be removed and burned. Finally as an outlaw, his head was cut off and placed on London Bridge, while the remainder of his body was to be cut into quarters to be displayed in Newcastle, Berwick, Sterling and Perth. As historian John Reuben Davies put it,

Wallace's execution is a classic scene from one of history's great tragedies the death of a national hero, a bloodthirsty judicial killing the demonstrative and exemplary justice of an English King. A plaque now documents the spot near where he was executed on August 23 1305. After the Treaty of Edinburgh Northampton in 1328, Scotland began the 1330s in a fairly good position.

Almost three decades of civil war and war with England had severely sapped the country's resources and morale. However, Robert the Bruce had for the time being secured a peaceful end to the English coveting of Scotland. Bruce's Death On the seventh of June 1329, left behind a four year old son, David the second. David the second was crowned King of Scotland on 24 Nov.1329. And a guardianship was assumed by Thomas Randolph, who was then Earl of Murray. In England Edward the third was determined to avenge the humiliation of England by the Scots. Despite having signed the Treaty of Edinburgh, North Hampton, Edward the third was not the same man as his father, and though he was young, he had a similarly ambitious nature to that of his grandfather, Edward the first. Edward had not acted under his own initiative, having instead been pressured by Roger Mortimer, his Regent, as well as his mother, Isabella of France.

The peace of North Hampton, dubbed by the English as the shameful piece had failed to account for Reparations to a group of nobles, who held land and estates in both England and Scotland. Their properties and titles had been given to Bruce's allies, an act that still sat sourly with both the English nobility and Edward the third. England was suffering from a depleted Treasury following the wars waged against Scotland. Yet the outraged English people and its King were in no position to attempt any further action against Scotland by them. In 1330, the year following the coronation of David the second saw two events occur, which would prove to be significant for both Edward and the future of Scotland. Edward the third had his regent Roger Mortimer executed, thus taking full control of his crown and country. Secondly, Edward Bailio made an appeal to the now unbridled English King. The previous King of Scotland, John Bailio, who after the English invasion of Scotland in 1296, had been forced to abdicate his throne had left behind a son, Edward Bailio. Edward Bailio approach the King of England, wanting the return of ancestral lands that he claimed was rightfully his.

Before the end of the year, Edward the third sent demands to young King David's Regent Thomas Randolph, Randolph delayed responding, despite Edward the third pressing the matter, with the second request on 22 April 1332. Meanwhile Bailio and his followers began to prepare for an invasion of Scotland. The Battle of Duplinmore was to be the opening skirmish in what would become known as the second war of Scottish independence. The battle was a significant opener to the war, one which was won by Edward Bailio and Commander Henry DE Beaumont. To circumvent the terms of the Treaty of North Hampton, the Scottish rebels and their English allies sailed from several ports in Yorkshire to the king horn in Fife, on the 31st of July 1332. The terms of the treaty did not permit English forces to cross the tweed. From King Horn they eventually marched to Perth. On the 10th of August, the army was camped at For Teviot, a few miles short of the much stronger force led by Donald the Earl of Mar, which was positioned on the heights of Duplinmore.

A second Scottish force led by Patrick Earl of Dunbar was fast approaching Bailio's army from the rear. The predicament led to no courage to the smaller army, and morale and Bailio's camp began to shrink. Henry Beaumont, the commander of Bailio's army, was accused by the other disinherited lords, claiming he had betrayed them through false promises of Scottish support for Bailio once they had entered Scotland. Beaumont, by far the most experienced soldier on either side, reacted with cool precision, ordering his troops to risk crossing the river earn at night and launching a surprise attack on the enemy before they could link with the approaching second force. Overconfident of his superior force, Donald the Earl of Mar, ordered his army to settle down on the night of 10 August, not bothering to set a watch. At midnight under the cover of darkness, and with no guard present from the opposing army to raise the alarm Beaumont Bailio's force across the urn to take up a defensive position on high ground at the head of a narrow valley, outflanking Mar. With the rapid approach of the main Scottish force Beaumont knew that the time to act was now. The army formed aligns, with archers on each flank and men at arms at the center, resembling a quarter moons.

The Scots, angry that their enemy had out-maneuvered them, charged up the defensively formed English army in disorganized shieldtrins, all formation lost to the reckless charge. Mars wild charge was met with a hail of arrows, falling on the Scottish flanks. The unarmed Scottish footmen with unvisered helmets were ill prepared for the volley of arrows which fell murderously, thinning their ranks in heartbeats. The superior force however, was able to get through the storm of arrows and meet the center of the English force, where Beaumont's men at arms finally gave some ground but the unrelenting barrage of arrows thinned out the charging armies' flanks, forcing them to push into the middle to escape the reign of death. The larger force lost all ability to maneuver and the crowded middle ranks of the army were pushed into the waiting Spears of the English. The Scottish dead were piled high as the battle ended with the English surrounding the mass of bodies. The Scots losses were heavy. Mar himself was killed, as were several other key members of the Scottish army. Estimates and between two and 13,000 Scottish dead against relatively light English losses had marked the first battle of the second war for Scottish independence. And not since the Battle of Fall Kirk and the Scottish felt such a terrible defeat.

The worst casualty of all was the loss of national confidence that had grown through the successive victories of King Robert Bruce. Dunbar's army was still in the field of a similar number to Mars prior to his defeat. However, the confidence of Bailio and Beaumont's troops sword. The decimation of Mars troops was felt through the arriving army. Dunbar was reluctant to engage the force that had so thoroughly dispatched one of equal size to his. The English would learn from this battle most keenly and the formation adopted by the Bailio and Beaumont would become a standard battle order one which would provide England with many future victories. The decisive victory granted valuable time to Edward Bailio's invasion, also leaving him well placed in Scotland to gather supporters and swell his ranks. Bailio saw particularly strong support from the residents of Fife and Straightern. Not long after his victory at Dunbar, Bailio was crowned the king of Scots, a title he used to gain further support as his army marched across the country, eventually settling in Rocks Borough. While at Rocks Borough, with his forces swelling due to the spreading news of his victory against the usurpers and claim to the throne. Bailio offered his loyalty to Edward the third, pledging to support all of Edwards's future battles as well as offering to wed David the second sister. A move that would further legitimize his claim to the throne and expand his lands and fortunes.

Bailio then left Rocks Borough moving on to Anand, which would be the site of the chemist's aid of Anand, a battle between the supporters of Bailio and the loyalist troops of David the second led by Sir Archibald Douglas and John Randolph, third Earl of Murray. Bailio would lose this battle to the Bruce loyalists, but managed to escape fleeing Scotland to return to Edward in England. Meanwhile, David the second own resistance had been thrown into turmoil at the death of Thomas Randolph his regent. Thomas had been a constant companion to Robert to Bruce in his final years and taken over management of Bruce's household. Robert had decreed before his death that Randolph would serve as David's Regent, a role he performed wisely and with honor before his unfortunate death at Muscle Borough. Randolph had been on his way to engage Edward Bailio and his supporters when he died. Many believed it to be the result of English poison, but the most likely culprit was a kidney stone.

Once he had returned to England, Edward Bailio once again offered his loyalty and homage to Edward the third, requesting his aid in the combined campaign against Scotland. Bailio returned to Scotland in March 1333 to lay siege to Berwick upon tweed. Berwick upon tweed held a strategic position on the border between Scotland and England, being the main route for both invasion and trade. The town had a tumultuous past, having been sacked by Edward the first in 1296, one of the first actions which marked the beginning of the first

Scottish War of Independence. Edward the third justification of the military actions against Berwick upon tweed, and the violation of the Treaty of Northampton was due to his claims that Scotland was preparing for war.

His incursion being a response to threats from the North. Bailio cross the border first with his disinherited Scottish Lords on 10 March, accompanied by some English magnates. Edward had invested heavily in the nobles accompanying the campaign, providing grants of over 1 million pounds to the Englishman, and similar amounts to Bailio and his Scottish nobles.

Bailio's army reached Berwick in late March and immediately made moves to encircle the town and cutting off all aid by land. Edwards Navy having already done the same by Sea. Edward himself arrived at Berwick with the bulk of the English army on the ninth of May, some six weeks after Bailio had arrived and laid siege. Bailio had not been idle, unleashing a scorched earth policy upon the surrounding lands, ensuring that there was little to no sustenance in the region to resupply the town if the opportunity arose. The town's water supply had already been cut, trenches dug, and all communication out of Berwick was made impossible while Edwards accompanying craftsmen began work on the siege engines required to take the town.

A large Scottish army was gathering just north of the border under the leadership of Sir Archibald Douglas. He concentrated his energy on swelling the ranks of the army, rather than utilizing the troops he already had, except for carrying out some minor rating into Cumberland. Unfortunately, these raids had little effect in drawing the English away from Berwick and instead provided Edward with justification for his military campaign. By the end of June with the full support of the English army, it's tribuchais and catapults and also Edwards Navy Berwick was close to falling. With its garrison exhausted and half the town destroyed a truce was requested by the defending commander Alexander Seton.

Edward agreed to the truce on the condition that Seton surrenders by 11 July. Douglas was now without options, and the army that had gathered north of the border was compelled into action. Douglas had approximately 13,000 troops, significantly more than Edwards 9000. On the last day of Seton's truce, the army entered England marching to the port of tweed mouth. The little port had been destroyed. Having been an obstacle for the large Scottish army, who were eager to provide the relief required by the truce set down by Edward? A few hundred Scottish cavalry were able to navigate their way across the ruins of the old bridge, and then force their way to Berwick. In their minds and in those of the Scottish garrison at Berwick. The terms of the truce had been satisfied. Edward argued that the relief was to have come from Scotland, or rather the direction of Scotland. While the few hundred Scottish cavalry had entered Berwick from the English side.

After much arguing a fresh truce was agreed to on the provision of relief before the 20th of July.

Douglas knew that a foray against England in his current defensive position would be disastrous, even with a superior numbers. To draw the English army out to more favorable terrain Douglas Marched the Scottish army south towards Bambra, threatening to besieged the town where Edwards Queen was currently in residence. However, Edward was confident in Bambra' defenses, and the Scots had not the time to construct the type of machinery needed to breach the fortress. Instead, the Scottish army ravaged the countryside. Edward ignored this, positioning his army on Haledon Hill, a highly defensive position on a rise of some 600 feet. Douglas out of options had little choice but to engage Edward on the ground of his choosing. To engage the English army the Scots descended downhill to the marshy ground that covered the area before Haledon Hill. Once over the marshy ground, they still had the hill to climb before reaching the English forces. The journey left the Scottish Spearman vulnerable to English arrows for a long period of time without cover. Casualties were heavy. However, the survivors made it to the crest of the hill, climbing towards the waiting Spears of the English. The Scottish army broke. Their casualties were in the thousands including Douglas himself. Edwards's casualties were numbered at just 14.

The next day Berwick's truce expired, and the towns surrendered to Edwards's terms. The loss of Douglas and the troops at Haledon Hill was a tremendous blow to the supporters of David the second. The Scottish King would soon be exiled to France, where he would remain until 1341. Edward Bailio was crowned and quickly fulfilled his promises to Edward. Acknowledging fealty and subjection to Edward, Bailio surrendered Berwick as an inalienable possession of the English crown. Following Later that year, Bailio also yielded Rocks Pearl, Edinburgh, Pebels, Dumfries, Linlithgow and Headington and though Edward did not remove Scottish laws, he did replace the men in charge with his own. While David the second was removed, and Edward the third attended to the issues of his own kingdom, Bailio was troubled by unrest among both the Scottish nationalists and his own allies. While Bailio's allies seemed to be deserting him, his enemies were only growing in number. He retired to Berwick, managing to convince Edward the third that the situation was under control. Though In the meantime, more and more of his men were defecting to join those loyal to David the second.

French and English relations were already tense but Philip the second to France offered shelter to David the second. A mutual defensive pact had been signed between Scotland and France in 1295 under the then King John Bailio, Edward Bailio's father. After a plea for aid from David's new co regions, Philip sent an ambassador to England to discuss the recent events between Scotland and England. Unfortunately, not much would be gained by the ambassadors, who failing to make headway with the disorganized members of Edward the second loyalist's supporters only succeeded in unwittingly allowing England time to recover their finances. In March 1335, having lost confidence in Bailio's ability to hold sway over the Scottish nobleman, Edward began mustering his forces, Scotland was aware of the growing mobilization of English forces and began to quietly prepare. Edward raised his largest army to date, number 13,000 men. His strategy a three pronged invasion of Scotland. Bailio would take troops west from Berwick. While Edward led his troops north from Carlyle and a naval force near the Clyde would form the third front of the invasion. The armies encountered little resistance, meeting up at Glasgow and eventually settling in the area of Perth.

In France, an army of 6000 soldiers was openly assembled to aid the Scottish troops. Edward was informed that these troops would be deployed if he did not submit to arbitration by France and the Pope. Edward refused. Meanwhile, Scottish loyalist forces were not faring well. Andrew Murray agreed to a truce with Edward lasting from October until Christmas. However Bailio and his followers were not included in the terms. Bailio through the support of David the third Streth Boogie, laid siege against Kildromi Castle.

Murray sent troops after him routing his force and killing

Streth Boogie. Bailio would see many more defeats in the coming years that would force him to rely more and more heavily on the English King.

In May 1336, Edward pushed on with his invasion plans despite the threat from the French. He received reports of the massing forces of Philip and intended to block the most likely port of arrival, Aberdeen. Edward moved from Newcastle, with the force of 400 men swelling his ranks as he marched on Lockingdorm ending Scottish sieges and destroying everything he encountered before burning Aberdeen to the ground. The English embassy had been attempting to negotiate with Philip the sixth and David the second. However, in August, they received final word from Philip. His invasion of England would proceed. French privateers attacked the town of Oxford also capturing several royal ships. Edward received word of French actions by September. He abandoned his immediate plans in Scotland and returned to England. However, he was too late to strike back at French ships. He raised funds before returning to Scotland, settling down to winter at the fortress in Clyde after a series of wins and losses. Scotland was under heavy strain, with both English and Scottish forces ravaging the countryside, each trying to eliminate any advantage the other force might acquire.

Disease and hunger were rampant among the people. The Scottish loyalists used the French distractions to their advantage, and by the end of March, they had reclaimed most of Scotland north of the fourth and had dealt serious blows to lands owned by Edward Bailio. Edward the third was forced to focus on France vowing to return to Scotland once they had been taken care of. In the meantime France had also continued to pour supplies into Scotland to aid the Scottish loyalists. The newly provisioned Scottish forces were able to progress further south and into northern England, laying waste to Cumberland and forcing Edward to split his efforts between both French and Scottish threats. Early winter of 1338 was seen as a turning point for the Scots and though the ruthless actions of Murray had left such devastation in his own lands that thousands of Scottish people were left without a means to feed themselves. He had effectively ended the possibility for Edward the third to establish a stable lordship over southern Scotland.

Chapter 5: The Black Death

After killing millions as it spread westward from China and throughout the Mediterranean. The Black Death devastated England between 1348 and 1349. Deaths were caused by a combination of fatal airborne diseases. The bubonic plague during the summer months, the pneumonic plague during winter and possibly anthrax. Modern scientific studies attribute the infection to the bacterium you're Sinia pesto. This strain is ancestral to all currently existing why pesto strains, but there is also evidence to indicate that it may have had viral origins. The inhabitance of medieval Europe believed that the plague was airborne, but scientists believe that it actually spread on the backs of Rodin's, primarily rats, which were surreptitiously infested with plague carrying fleas. London was hit in September, 1348 with the entirety of East Anglia affected the following year. Whales and the Midlands were infected by the spring of 1349. That summer it spread across the Irish Sea and penetrated northward into Scotland.

Historians believed that the Scots had been infected because they chose to attack various English towns as they were succumbing to the plague, believing that the disease was retribution from God. Nearly 5,000 Scottish soldiers fielded a botched attempt to invade England. Scotland did not suffer as much as it's Western European counterparts because of its cooler climate and more dispersed population. Even so, the plague was capable of wiping out the majority of the urban populations based in cities like Glasgow and Edinburgh. An English account of the pandemic reveals that even small villages were not fully spared from its deadly embrace. Sometimes it came by road, passing from village to village, sometimes by river as in the East Midlands or by ship, from the Low Countries or from other infected areas. On the villas of the bishop of [02:13 inaudible] states in the West Midlands, they, the death rates ranged between 19% of manorial tenants at Whortleberry and Hanbury to no less than 80% at Aston.

It is very difficult for us to imagine the impact of plague on these small rural communities. Where a village might have no more than 400 or 500 inhabitants. From the world upside down in Black Death in England, J Bolton. Apart from the mystery of its origins and how it spread, the Black Death was so terrifying because of the speed in which it struck and the scale of its activity. Entire villages could be wiped out in a matter of days. While large urban areas could easily lose between 80 to 90% of their populations. The exact number of Scottish people that died due to the plague is unknown, but historians estimate that about a fifth of Scotland's population was lost during this time. Approximately 1 million people. Even this conservative estimate is enough to make it the most fatal calamity in the history of the kingdom. The very small minority who survived an infection had to live the rest of their lives with crippling mental and physical disabilities.

The first signs that someone had been infected were usually the emergence of lumps in the armpits or groin. After that, angry black spots began to appear on the thighs, arms, and other parts of the body. This was typically a death sentence within three days. The colder Scottish climate deterred the bubonic form of the plague, but it allowed the pneumonic or septicemia plague to achieve a high death toll. The nobles were often spared by virtue of their isolation in the castles, but the middle and lower classes were mostly unable to escape its ravages. To make matters worse, the plague was not a one off phenomenon. Instead it returned to haunt Scotland multiple times throughout the subsequent centuries. The final outbreak occurred in the 1640s. It stifled all aspects of life from the economic to the political, to the cultural. Children whose parents were dying from the plague, refused to visit their death beds out of fear of becoming infected themselves.

There was a shortage of labor leaving many farms, unmanned for years. Many fields were allowed to rot, reversing all the agricultural and manufacturing progress that had been achieved after the wars of independence finally came to an end. Wars were halted as were much of international and international trade. Combating the plague certainly took its toll on Scotland. In the 17th century. It finally managed to return to pre plague population levels. This was achieved by the implementation of strict health controls whenever an outbreak occurred, people were prohibited from gathering, and those believed to be infected, were placed in quarantine. The foul cleansers were widely employed in Edinburgh and other Scottish towns by this time. Their job was to relocate plague victims far away from human settlements to die and to burn all their homes, clothes, and possessions to the ground.

Chapter 6: How Scotland Was Built Into An Industrial Economy By Inventors, Explorers, And Missionaries

In the early 1700s, Scotland was mostly a rural and agricultural economy. It had only a population of 1 million people with a relatively small portion based in its modern urban townships. Within the course of a single lifetime, everything changed. By the 1820s the effects of the Industrial Revolution were unmistakable. The scientific theories that had been conceptualized during the Scottish Enlightenment swiftly turned into practical applications that could be turned into hardy profits in a capitalist world. Scotland's population rose dramatically, people left the countryside and traditional farm life for manufacturing towns, which eventually became bustling cities.

There were approximately 1.5 million people in Scotland during the start of the 19th century. By the end of the 20th century, this number had tripled to over 4.5 million people. A significant portion of this rise can be attributed to immigrants, particularly Irish immigrants, who were fleeing the prospect of starvation during the Irish Potato Famine 1845 to 1849. This population rise was also partly the byproduct of crucial advancements in medicine, health care and public health standards. These improvements reduced the mortality rate in the face of previously fatal epidemic diseases. Meanwhile, the scientific innovations that were assimilated into traditional agricultural practices allowed fewer farmers to produce enough produce to feed a larger population. South Eastern farmers were praised for their efficiency. Northeastern farmers for their cattle and beef and Airsher a county in the southwest for the large quantities of quality milk their cows produced.

Innovations in chemistry, for example, the use of chlorine to bleach linen, helped make the Scottish textile industry surpass agriculture. Linen production became more efficient than ever before, with the use of newly discovered chemicals and the adoption of English inventions, like Hargreaves, spinning jenny, argrites water frame, and Crompton's mule. These inventions transformed the weaving process, radically increasing output, productivity and competitiveness. Instead of relying on human power alone, these new spinning machines were powered by massive water wheels. The old tradition of men working on hand blooms was replaced by an efficient factory system. Women and children were roped into the workforce spending long hours toiling for relatively low wages.

During the 1830s heavy Industry replaced textiles as the most important component of the Scottish economy. The production of coal and iron rose tremendously, facilitating the popularization of railways, steam locomotives and ships. The use of canals and horses as the dominant form of transportation slowly became obsolete. If the first phase of the Industrial Revolution mainly consisted of old industries becoming more efficient through the adoption of new technologies. The second phase was driven by Scottish innovations themselves. Henry Bell 1767 to 1830 built the comet, the first successful passenger steamship in 1812. It catalyzed the birth of the Scottish shipbuilding industry and the railway industry. James Watt 1736 to 1819 did not invent the steam engine as commonly believed. It had existed since the early 18th century, but he did invent the separate condenser, which reduced the amount of water steam engines needed while allowing them to produce more power.

The introduction of an extensive railway network helped Scotland to make significant economic progress during the Victorian era. When Queen Victoria assumed the throne in 1827, there were only a few Scottish railway lines in existence. These were mainly used to transport coal and other industrial raw materials between the bustling urban hubs of Glasgow, Edinburgh and Dundee. In 1843 the Edinburgh Glasgow railway line opened, catalyzing a national obsession with railways. Within a single generation practically all of Scotland's railways were built, constituting some of the world's most ambitious engineering projects at the time. Railway tracks were built between small villages and major towns stretching across all directions. Thanks to the advent of efficient steam engines, journeys that would have taken days on horse drawn carriages were now completed in a matter of hours. There was, of course, a dark side to all this intellectual, economic and technological progress. The extensive railway network effectively bridge the distance between the urban centers and the countryside, allowing tourism in rural Scotland to boom.

Urban growth during the Victorian era had created dirty, overcrowded and polluted cities. With Glasgow being the primary example. The lack of adequate housing for the large influx of migrants had led to the sprawl of slums with dire standards of living. With over 20,000 people forced to live in shabby housing and practically no sanitation. One can only imagine the effect of such conditions on the body and mind. These dismal living conditions were incredibly conducive to disease. Glasgow soon became a hotbed for typhus and typhoid. Scotland's participation in the global British Empire also led to a deadly outbreak of cholera. In 1832 the first cholera outbreak in Scotland killed 3000 people in Glasgow alone. All the public health advances that had been achieved since the black plague were temporarily reversed as death rates soared to 17th century heights. It appears obvious now, but the link between dirt and disease was not immediately apparent then. It was only after the subsequent color epidemics of 1848 and 1853 that the medical community identified the filthy living conditions as a problem that had to be solved.

The introduction of an expensive sewage system and a clean water supply from Lock Katrine from 1850 and 1875 was crucial in improving sanitation and public health standards in Glasgow. Eager to escape the grimness of city life, many wealthier Scots took the opportunity to breathe in the fresh air and enjoy the stunning vistas of the Scottish countryside. They also developed appetites for hunting deer, shooting birds and fishing. By the 1890s there were widespread concerns that urban rural tourism was devastating the countryside and causing various species of bird and deer to tether towards extinction. Apart from the rising pollution levels, and the desecration of nature for the extraction of raw materials, Scotland's relentless appetite for wealth and progress incurred heavy ethical costs. As Scotland looked beyond its traditional trading relationships with France and the Low Countries, Netherlands, Belgium and Western Germany, it became complicit in the impure exploitation of countries and populations outside of Europe.

The Scottish textile industry developed a dependence on imported cotton from India, England's prized colonial possession as well as the slave plantations of America. Scottish capitalists also proved to be adept at extracting profits from the Atlantic trade of tobacco. There were no tobacco plantations in Scotland. But Glasgow's infamous tobacco Lords were able to gain a firm grip on the trade through their strategic position. Glasgow was closer to the transatlantic shipping routes than London or Bristol and Saby use of capital. Their agents sailed out to North Carolina and Virginia to trade with the owners of small tobacco plantations. They provided credit and loaned them tools brought from Scottish iron and Scottish made linen, which would be repaid with takings from their future crops.

As these plantations grew in size and scale with the help of their funding, so did the amount of tobacco that made its way to Glasgow's warehouses.

No ship that sailed into Glasgow needed to wait very long to be fully loaded with tobacco. Tobacco was only one component of Scotland's three way trade, with the rapidly evolving American economy. Ships from Scotland would sail to Africa to be filled with slaves. These slaves would then be taken to either tobacco plantations in America or sugar plantations in the West Indies. The ships would return to Scottish ports with the products of this exploitative labor system, primarily sugar and tobacco. This arrangement also brought in large amounts of profits into

Scotland, which could then be reinvested into the Scottish Industrial Revolution. In 1747, the tobacco Lords became even wealthier when the French government gave Glasgow a lucrative monopoly over the supply of tobacco to France. The huge influx of money into Scotland's rising number of banks facilitated the growth of a financial industry and newfangled forms of credit.

Chapter 7: Problems Facing Scotland Today

The powers in question involve matters of broad national concern, such as food safety laws, public service recruitment and environmental laws. The Scottish Parliament is concerned that Westminster may compromise Scottish interests in its desperation to strike up a trade deal with United States President Donald Trump. A prospect that could easily materialize if Westminster can sideline the Scottish Parliament from the decision making table. This situation also exemplifies the fact that the Westminster Parliament only holds its sovereignty as a matter of principle. The interest of the Scottish, the Welsh and the Northern Irish are purely secondary. Scottish First Minister Nicola Sturgeon has noted that her government would in good faith and a spirit of compromise. Seek to identify a solution that might enable Scotland's voice to be heard and mitigate the risks that Brexit poses to our interests within the UK.

Sturgeon has pointed out that the majority of Scottish voters opted to remain in the EU, and that access to the European single market was crucial. If Scotland cannot remain as a full member of the EU post Brexit, then the option may be to seek full independence. One option in my view, the best option, is to become a full member of the EU as an independent country.

Indeed, independence would resolve the fundamental cause of the position Scotland currently finds itself in. Westminster governments that Scotland doesn't vote for imposing policies that the majority in Scotland does not support. This is undoubtedly the boldest of options, especially since the United Kingdom is a far more significant trade partner than the EU.

In 2016, exports to the rest of the UK accounted for 61%, 45.8 billion pounds of total Scottish exports, while exports to the EU only accounted for 17% of total exports, 12.7 billion pounds. Scotland's interests in maintaining ties with Europe are thus not purely materialistic. Sturgeon diplomatically contrasts the attractiveness of European ideals in contrast to Westminster's historical heavy handedness in dealing with Scotland. Europe is about more than economics. The European ideal is one of peaceful coexistence, mutual solidarity and support and prosperity built on cooperation. There is much still to achieve, but a Europe which encourages openness and civic dialogue and which welcomes difference is one from which Scotland has gained much into which it still wants to contribute.

His history and endless cycle or a series of progressions and regressions. The dilemma that sturgeon's government faces would certainly be familiar to many of Scotland's medieval kings, many of whom have actively sought fraternity with their counterparts in Europe as a means to neutralize the threat of their dominant southern neighbor. Sturgeon's emphasis on Europe welcoming difference hints at inalienable rights that the EU accords to its smaller members, beneath its countless rules and treaties, there is an acceptance of cultural and historical differences between its members. A reflection of the post-World War Two striving to avoid further conflicts between European nations. This acceptance of heterogeneity stands in contrast to the general pressure to conform and Anglicized according to English norms within the United Kingdom. The pragmatic benefits of a continued relationship with England and the United Kingdom as a whole remain. But this relationship is predicated on Scottish interests playing second fiddle to Westminster's.

Sturgeon herself has made it clear that she wishes for Scotland to finally wrestle its rights to complete autonomy. A desire to be free of Westminster that is akin to Westminster's own desire to be free of influence from Brussels, once and for all. Her patients indicate that she has a long term strategy in mind. After calling for a second referendum in 2016 after Brexit, which Theresa May denied, she obtained a good sense of Scotland's appetite for independence in the light of an impending loss of EU membership. A second referendum on Scottish independence after May has ironed out all the Brexit details with Brussels is imminent. In the meantime, Scotland looks inwards towards its various problems, social and economic inequality divisions between the Catholics and Protestants. Its economic prospects in the near future before contemplating her place in a politically volatile world.

Conclusion

With that, we have come to the end of this book. I want to thank you for choosing this book.

Now that you have come to the end of this book, we would first like to express our gratitude for choosing this particular source and taking the time to read through it. All the information here was well researched and put together in a way to help you understand the history of Scotland as easily as possible.

We hope you found it useful and you can now use it as a guide anytime you want. You may also want to recommend it to any family or friends that you think might find it useful as well.

Thanks!